# Toddler Potty Training

*The Guide For Modern Busy Parents to Potty-Train, Includes Positive Discipline and Basic Concept*

**Kate Cartes**

# Table of Contents

# Introduction

Potty-training is one of those process parents employ in use with their kids to help them in managing their bowel movements for the benefit of both the parent and the child in the long run. In potty-training, parents try to teach the child to correctly recognize and communicate when he/she needs to use the bathroom, to resist the former urge of defecating where they are, and to use the potty or toilet properly.

With the use of positive reinforcement and creative techniques, your child will have the confidence that they need in order to learn all of the necessary steps. This success comes from your child's willingness to participate and your open-minded approach. Getting rid of the pressure that surrounds the topic, you will learn if your child is ready by assessing their individual traits. It is important to remember that patience is the foundation of any milestone. The energy that you provide your child with is the energy that they are going to mirror. This is why staying calm and be patient is essential when you are potty-training. There are going to be some setbacks along the way, but if you are able to prepare yourself and your child adequately, you both will be able to overcome them with ease. Once you begin the process, you are already one step closer to achieving the potty-training goals. Potty training your children isn't generally a pretty activity. Without a doubt, children virtually get bothered, so you should be cautious. Pretty things dependably get kids' attention. Consequently, you should make striking things that would get their attention. Presenting the training dynamically will surely shield your children from getting tired.

Also, this book teaches you how to combine positive discipline with motivational coaching in the classroom. You'll use positive discipline once your child has been caught doing something wrong. Then, you can help them make a better choice in the future by showing them how their mistakes have consequences.

Positive discipline works for all ages of children, including preschoolers. This book will help you apply it in the classroom as well as at home. It covers many examples of what successful parents and teachers use to teach children.

Children come into being without instructions. It is up to parents to raise them properly, provide discipline, and ensure that they are well-provided. Every parent wants a well-behaved, happy, healthy, and respectful child. No one likes to raise spoiled brats, but sometimes children become too difficult to deal with, leaving parents frustrated and perplexed.

# CHAPTER 1:

## Troubleshooting

Potty-training is not always guaranteed to be a smooth ride. In most cases, there will be bumps in the road. It is therefore important to be prepared to face these challenges together with the kid. These problems may look unsolvable or get really frustrating, but with the right methods, you'll be over the training process in no time.

In this chapter, we'll examine a long list of common potty-training problems and the practical steps which you can take in solving them. However, if you suspect the problem is the result of a health issue, you can consult a medical professional to be safe.

## Common Issues and Solutions

### *What to Do If the Child is Afraid*

Anxiety is one of the major problems most parents face during potty-training which can be very crippling. The child may be suffering from general anxiety which reflects on the potty-training process or may be suffering from potty-training anxiety. Either way, it is important to face this problem head-on, as you won't be able to get anything done if your child is afraid.

First, you should identify the type of anxiety your child suffers from. If the child suffers from general anxiety, you can visit a therapist for diagnosis and treatment. There is a condition known as generalized anxiety disorder in which the kid worries about a variety of issues that should not be a source of worry normally. Below is an excerpt from a Boston Children's Hospital publication describing the condition.

Fear can make the child refuse to sit on a potty or toilet. Some children even get scared of making a bowel movement in the potty while some may be afraid of the toilet flushing. Anxiety can also cause the child to wet themselves or defecate in places you don't expect. It is very important to address these issues in the right way.

If the child is afraid of sitting on the potty or pooping in the potty chair, you should start by encouraging the child to sit on the potty periodically with clothes on at first, then with clothes off later. You can get them accustomed to the potty by decorating it with stickers together and getting toys which, the child can only play with when he sits on the potty. Make sure the potty is comfortable enough for the child. To help with this, let the child join you in shopping for the potty before you start potty-training. You should then pick the one the child chooses.

### The Child Has an Accident While Playing

It is quite common for a child to wet or soil themselves while playing, usually as a result of excitement or distraction. First, you should make sure it isn't a result of a medical issue such as incontinence or an overactive bladder.

Generally, children are not able to control their bladder until around the age of three or four. Even at that age, accidents are still common, especially during the night. Research shows that there is a link between the digestive system and the brain. The digestive tract has nerves that can be triggered by an emotional, exciting, or stressful event.

The child may get carried away playing and ignore the urge to ease themselves until it becomes uncontrollable or may simply wet themselves as a result of too much excitement or stimulation. To prevent this, you should help the child follow a consistent bathroom routine and to make sure he or she eases themselves before going out to play.

Potty accidents when playing could also be caused by constipation or by the child holding it in deliberately. The child may choose to hold it in either as a result of an emotional reaction or anxiety. However, accidents may then happen during play as the child gets too relaxed or too excited to control their bladder or bowel. When this happens, do not ignore the situation or yell at the child. Let the child calm down first and then proceed to clean the mess together. The child shouldn't return to playing until he has been cleaned up and the mess disposed of properly.

While the child is playing, you can also make them take short breaks to go to the bathroom. This will help in emptying his bladder and bowels and also to calm him down. You also can limit any adrenaline-inducing play in the meantime. Things such as throwing the child up or swinging them around can cause an adrenaline spike or a bit of fear, thereby making the child lose control of their bowels and bladder.

Though potty accidents can be frustrating, you should keep in mind that accidents while playing are normal during potty-training and are a result of a natural response to excitement or anxiety. Since the child is still developing, issues such as this may occur frequently but the child should grow out of it with age. However, if this gets too severe or continues till over the age of five, it is advisable to visit a medical professional.

***Your Child Doesn't Want to Go to the Bathroom with You***
Your child may refuse to go to the bathroom with you or anyone else present. This isn't unusual. At a period, children start to develop a sense of awareness and they start being conscious of their body. During this period, the child will begin to desire privacy all of a sudden. The child may refuse to go to the bathroom with you or anyone also as a way of showing independence. You must therefore be prepared to handle this carefully as a parent.

It is good to respect a child's boundaries as a parent, but what if your child isn't capable of using the bathroom on his or her own? Leaving the child unsupervised in this case will lead to lots of cleaning for you. What you should do is explain to the child why he or she can't get the privacy they want yet. They have to learn how to use the potty or toilet, to wipe themselves and flush, and also how to wash their hands. If they learn how to do these properly, they'll have the freedom to use the bathroom on their own. This will serve as extra motivation for the child to learn the process faster.

From another point of view, your child may simply be self-conscious or may be ashamed of his body. You should check for any signs of abuse, either physical or emotional. A child getting ashamed of his or her body suddenly may be a sign of abuse. Do visit a therapist if the child's behavior gets suspicious.

You should teach the child right from the start that there's nothing wrong with his/her body. Do not make fun of any of his physical attributes. This can affect the child's self-esteem negatively. If the child is uncomfortable with you being with him or her in the bathroom, you can ask a family member of the same gender to accompany them.

The child may refuse your company in the bathroom also as a way of showing independence. This is okay but you should make sure he or she has learned the process properly. Let them recite the steps to take until you are satisfied. You can remind them of what he or she should do while they are inside to be safe. Pediatric psychologists have explained that it is important for the child to create boundaries around his or her body as the child starts gaining independence and self-awareness.

Respecting your child's boundaries will go a long way in creating a sense of self-respect and improving the child's self-esteem. This will also teach the child to respect other people's boundaries as children learn through imitation. However, you should teach the child to be open with you and to feel free to talk about any issue.

### *The Child Poops Next to the Potty*

You may have gotten your child to stop going in his or her underwear but you may be faced with another problem — the child misses when he or she tries to poop in the potty or poops next to it instead. To stop this, you should first observe the child to determine why he does it. There could be many reasons for this, so you have to get the specific cause. From my experience as a parent, I'll list the major reasons why a child "misses" or may poop next to the potty deliberately.

First, you may have trained your child to stop using diapers or going in his or her underwear, but the child may not be used to the potty yet. They know they shouldn't poop in their underwear but may be scared of using the potty. They then choose to poop next to the potty instead. That's why it is important to get your child familiar with the potty chair as soon as you start potty-training.

Encourage him or her to sit on the potty at frequent intervals; also, make sure he or she is comfortable sitting on the potty. You can motivate with toys and children's books. Praise them if they eventually poop inside the potty. If accidents occur, clean up the mess and let them see you put it inside the potty. They'll eventually learn that poop should always go in the potty.

Also, if the potty isn't easily accessible, accidents may happen. Children have a hard time correctly recognizing the urge to go beforehand, so the child may be hard-pressed before he eventually decides to use the potty. However, if he or she can't get to the potty on time, they may no longer be able to hold it in, thereby causing him or her to poop close to the potty instead. You should make sure that the potty chair is placed where the child can reach it easily. After getting a suitable location, make sure the potty is placed there consistently. As we've said many times, you should make sure your child's underwear and clothes are easily removable. This will help your child get to the potty on time as precious time won't be wasted on trying to get his clothes off. If it's too late for the child to hold it in, he may poop just before he sits on the potty.

With all that has been said, it is important to motivate the child too. Don't get worked up if he poops next to the potty instead of in it. When this happens, calmly correct them and motivate them to do better next time. Let him or her know you appreciate their effort in trying to use the potty instead of going in his underwear. Be patient with the child. Potty-training doesn't last forever, and you'll be over it in no time.

# CHAPTER 2

# Common Queries and Their Answer

## "Is It Better To Start Potty Training an Infant (Under 12 Months) or A Toddler?"

It will all depend on your family and your preferences as a parent. Some people will argue that they would prefer to potty train their infant child (when they are 12 months old or younger); however, I would personally say that I think it's better to start when your child is a toddler.

Children will start walking when they are 12, 16, or even 20 months of age; so, if your child cannot walk yet, you will have to take him or her to the potty all the time. To me, potty training comes as a gradual and natural thing; so, your child will start eating solids, then they will move on to crawling and walking, and to saying a couple of words, then they will eventually reach the potty training milestone. If you start potty training when your toddler is well, a toddler will also allow you to see how they react towards your stimulus (because you are showing them how to go potty).

You will also see if your toddler gives you any cues (such as doing a funny dance every time they need to go potty). Lastly, you will have a clearer picture of how to do potty training because your toddler is more likely to comprehend how they transition.

## "My Toddler Refuses To Go Potty. How Can I Help Her To Go Without Too Much Complaining?"

You will first need to become very patient and keep it up throughout their process! Your child doesn't know what the potty is, even if they see it all the time. They have spent most (if not all) of their lives wearing a piece of cloth or plastic that covers their parts; subsequently, they don't know what it's like to pee or poop without having something that will 'catch' their pee or poop.

Your toddler may not be aware that they need to go potty or are afraid of going potty because they do not feel comfortable enough. You will need to tell them to go potty continuously, and you will also need to go potty with them consistently. There is a new habit you are helping your toddler have, so it is essential to show them how, and eventually, they will follow without complaining.

## "My Child Hides Every Time He Needs to Poop, Is That Normal?"

Unfortunately for our parents, yes, there is normal behavior. And I say unfortunately because it is terrible when you are smelling poop, and you cannot find your toddler! 'How can they hide so fast without us seeing them!?' They do so because they may feel like being private about their actions or because they think you won't notice what they are doing.

Their type of behavior may make you feel like there isn't a light at the end of the tunnel. However, there is a way out! You will need to become more alert when your child sends subtle signals of needing to go potty. It's like you become mama-hawk or papa-hawk and observing your child thoroughly. They won't hide because you have caught their cues, and now you are taking them to the potty.

## "My Toddler Was Completely Potty Trained, and Now She Is Wetting Her Pants All the Time Again; What Can I Do About There?"

You need to see potty training as a process instead of as a "one-time event." There means that there may be times when your toddler reverts to wetting herself or not letting you know when she needs to go.

It would be best if you looked out for signs because perhaps something is going on around your daughter, making her go back on her process. Did you recently move to a new house? Does she have a new brother or sister on the way? Are you, as parents, going through a difficult time? These things could seriously affect your child's potty training journey.

However, you could quickly help her realize their new behavior by speaking candidly to her. It would help if you had a greater insight into what is going on inside your daughter's mind and why she is now acting their way; there will also help you understand and help her. For example, if there is a new baby on the way, make sure you spend as much time as possible with your daughter so that she won't feel jealous of her brother or sister.

Setting Up Your Daily Routine

Now that you have decided which tools you are going to invest in, you will also want to take some time to observe your child's behavior in preparation for creating your basic potty routine. There's no need to set alarms or stick to rigid schedules in the beginning. In fact, over-prompting can backfire and cause your little one to reverse course quickly.

You will want to take note over about a week when your child usually dirties a diaper and then prompt your child to go to the potty before those times. Initially, you will want to prompt your child to go at key times of the day, plus the times you note. The key times are usually around transition times like waking up, after meals, before leaving the house, arriving home, and before bed. Generally, your child should have the opportunity to go roughly once every 30–60 minutes in the beginning to increase the number of successes he or she will have. After a few days, you may notice a pattern on what times your child is using the potty most. Use these times as your new prompt times and continue to go if your child states an additional need.

You will see the number of trips to the bathroom naturally decrease. Soon enough, your child will recognize the urge to go and will start informing you reliably when the need arises. This will effectively eliminate the need to watch the clock overall, but you will still want to use your transition points (after meals, as soon as you get home from a shopping trip, etc.) as a reminder to at least try to sit on the potty.

In the beginning, you will also want to keep your child very well hydrated. Load up on morning liquids and then gradually decrease as the day goes on. Your child will learn faster if there are more opportunities for success. You want to purposefully cue that feeling quite often as you start training your toddler. Conversely, you don't want to have a big accident while your child sleeps. This is why you should taper off liquids later in the day. Try not to give your child any liquids within an hour of bedtime.

Be consistent in your approach to potty training. Your child is relying on you to help them be successful. If you happen to be out at the store and your little one indicates that it's time to go to the potty, it is best to drop everything and go. In time, you will get a little bit more time to get to the bathroom, but in the beginning, you may have very little time at all. This is one of the reasons why many people choose to spend the first few days or even the first week at home. There is nothing wrong with staying close to home in the beginning, but using a public restroom is part of the training and development that needs to occur. While you can do it later, it may actually be preferable to introduce this event earlier, especially because it requires your child to repeat the success at home into other locations. Some children have a tough time announcing the need to go potty in public, but you need to help your child overcome that hurdle because accidents in public are far more embarrassing and can cause your child to regress back to wanting to wear a diaper.

Your routine should also focus specifically on your little one's daytime potty habits. While some methods might advocate for putting daytime and nighttime training together, this is usually only successful with older children (36+ months), mostly due to physical development. For this reason, you will want to continue to use diapers or pull-ups overnight.

Part of your child's routine also needs to include fostering independence throughout the potty process. Ideally, you want your child to be completely self-sufficient while washing and drying hands or pulling pants on or off. In the beginning, though, your child will look to you for help. Using a visual chart for a reminder of what to do is one sure way to help your child get in and out of the bathroom more independently. This is important because, eventually, when it's time for your child to use the potty at night, you won't want to have to wake up to take them just to help with one step of the process like drying his or her hands or pulling up pants.

Likewise, you want to minimize your time interacting in the potty process, but if your child needs help, prompt them to ask for it. This will allow you to stay a little bit more removed from the actual activity and not end up with your child just relying on you to take care of their need. For example, if your child has gone in the potty and is having trouble wiping afterward but hasn't asked you for help, you might say something like, "Good job going potty! Do you need help wiping?"

Sometimes, a child gets frustrated and just stops trying or starts to cry. This is a good time to simply ask, "Can you ask for help?" This way your toddler starts to understand that you aren't going to simply take over when things get tough. At certain times of the day, you may find an extra need for help, especially at times when your child is tired.

There is one aspect of the potty routine that only affects boys. The age-old question of do we teach him to sit or stand to pee? Again, this is an area where you can use your best judgment, but many moms will tell you that it's far less messy if you teach a boy to sit to pee. Aiming is not only a skill, it takes a little concentration. Especially for younger boys, it's easy to be distracted or simply forget to aim, leaving you with a puddle to clean up and a frustrated child who didn't get it right.

A few other areas of consideration if you choose to have your child stand to pee are as follows:

How long will your son want to stand by the toilet? Sitting for 5 minutes is tough on a toddler; it can't be fun having to stand the whole time. It may actually feel like a punishment to a younger child.

What happens if your child is peeing and then needs to poop? Moving the toilet seat up or down quickly and not pinching fingers may be tricky to navigate without additional help.

What will your son do if he has to go into a public stall? Most stores don't have child-sized urinals or potties. This means your child will need to learn to sit anyway, at least until he is big enough to aim over the side of a standard height bowl without a stool.

What happens if he sees men standing to pee? In this case, if your son sees daddy standing to pee, he may very well want to try it too. It may then be difficult to get him to sit to pee. Quite frankly, if he is more interested in peeing while standing than sitting, you may have more success and easier time training. In this case, you may want to try using one of two tricks, bubbles, and targets.

If you don't have anything on hand to use as a target, or just don't feel right about throwing something into the toilet to pee on, then you can explain to your son that standing to pee requires that he aim for the middle of the bowl. He will know he did well if he makes bubbles in the water. On the other hand, if you don't mind tossing in a couple of fruit loops or cheerios, you can have him use them for target practice, which some boys really enjoy.

In either case, sitting to pee is still something your son will need to learn. You don't want to confuse him by going back and forth. So, if you find that your son is more successful standing to pee, go for it!

## Just Before You Begin

Once you have made your purchases and decisions about all these basic items to help your little one has an easier time learning to use the potty, it's time to put all your gear in place. For a few days leading up to actually starting to potty train, you'll want to spend time throughout the day talking about how fun it is to go potty and get rid of messy diapers. You will want to take a tour of the bathroom again, go over the picture chart, read potty books, sing songs, and make it sound like the biggest fun your child will have all year! Make sure you are modeling the behaviors you want your toddler to learn and invite them to sit on the potty next to you when you have to go, help you flush, and even wash hands for practice.

You will also want to have a quick chat with any child care providers because they will have to be included in this process. Let your provider know your expectations and the words you would like to use to communicate potty needs and ask them how you can accommodate them, such as providing a chart for them to help you keep track of your child's progress.

# CHAPTER 3:

## Common Challenges

There are quite a few challenges you might already expect, and then there are those that you might not know you could face while potty training your child.

### It's a Poop Thing

Sometimes, children might have a difficult time releasing poop. There could be a lot of reasons for this. Here are some of the reasons you can examine to see which one applies to your child.

- Could your child be constipated? When your child has constipation, make a note of the type of food you have been giving him or her, the food schedules (when you give your child breakfast, lunch, and dinner, and if you are also including certain snacks or juices), and food habits (does your child eat a lot or do you feel that he or she is eating less). Once you have the information, consult with your doctor so that you know what steps to take next. I met parents who had gone to the nearest pharmacy to get laxatives for children. Do not do that. Allow your doctor to recommend what steps to take next. You may not know if certain laxatives could have side effects on your child.

- Do they have unrealistic fears? You might notice that your children might begin to cry or show fear when they notice their poop. In such cases, you can use many techniques to alleviate their fears. You can use brown play-doh and drop it in the potty to show them that they have nothing to be scared of. Sometimes, children might be convinced that the poop is a part of their body and think something is getting separated from them. In such cases, bring out the teddy. I'm not kidding. One of the techniques that you can use is recommended by Dr. Phil (yes, THE Dr. Phil with his own show and his very recognizable face). In this method, you simply have to take a teddy and show your child how the teddy uses the potty. Make sure you are explaining to the child what is happening. You can use another soft toy, action figure, or even a doll to show this process to your child. Now I know that most people are rather skeptical about this process. However, I have met many parents who swear by this method.

- You might sometimes find that your child might begin to recognize pooping, but is still unable to recognize peeing. This is okay. Do not worry if your child learns to do one thing over the other. Continue with your potty training.

- Your child might be curious about the poop as well. He or she might attempt to touch it. Do not be upset by this behavior. We had seen earlier that your child could view poop as something that was part of them. This time, your child might just be wondering what this strange thing that appeared out of him or her is. You can prevent this habit by simply letting your child know that it is not something they should play with. Stay calm and don't make your child feel upset. Do not refer to poop as something dirty, as this could increase your child's fears and confusion.

- If you have family members, your significant other, caregivers, or even the staff at the daycare that can become involved in your child's potty training, or, if you simply want them to know about certain things regarding your child's potty training, then make sure you communicate it with them. It is better for everyone to be on the same page. This avoids confusion and prevents your child from learning different things from different people. When taking your child to daycare, you can explain your potty-training process to them. If they can help you with it, then that is awesome. You have help. However, if you think they are not being helpful, then you can use diapers when your child is in daycare. I know that many people suggest that you should never put the diaper back on when your child is being potty trained. However, as long as you are able to communicate with your child properly, this should not be a problem.

Regardless, I would recommend choosing to do something that you think is best for your child. Even when it comes to your family or significant other, make sure that they are indeed able to help you. If you think that their methods are only going to confuse your child, then you can have a conversation with them or have your child wear a diaper in their presence.

- Some children might become afraid when they see the toilets being flushed. They think that they might get sucked away. This is something you can easily work with. Give your child pieces of toilet paper and let them flush them. When they notice that the toilet paper gets flushed down but they are not sucked in, they begin to gain more confidence about using the flush.

- Regressions can be caused because of the unrealistic expectations that parents place on their children. Some of them become too fixated on the time period within which they would like to achieve results. For example, some parents might have read that children are usually potty trained anywhere between three to six months. To them, six months is the time limit that they place on their children. However, things don't work that way. Your child could master potty training within one month. Or your child could take longer than six months. Understand that potty training is a process that requires patience.

# How to Deal with Refusals

Your toddler is going to refuse to be potty trained. Do not panic or worry when that happens. These are things to be expected.

Let's answer the important questions first; why do children refuse or resist potty training?

There are numerous reasons, but the common one is that for children, things are about control. They like to handle things by themselves. When they see that potty training involves pooping, using the potty (which they are not familiar with), or even flushing (which might create ideas, such as the thought that the toilet is going to suck them), they might begin to feel that they are not in control. This causes them to be upset or be worried. Ever been in a situation where you tried telling your child to do something and their first response was a loud or stubborn NO? Your child is trying to exert control over certain things. They don't understand that some things are beyond their control.

It could also be that children cannot easily understand the instructions given to them by their parents. Potty training is a new concept, after all. It takes time for them to grasp what they should do and when. In such cases, they begin to resist going to the potty.

Other times, they are simply overwhelmed. They are experiencing new things and dealing with a lot of stimuli at one time. Our brains have been trained to ignore the trivial stuff. But the reason those things are trivial is that we have experienced them already. When you pass by a traffic light, for example, you might only look at it to see if you are supposed to stop or keep driving. Your child, on the other hand, is looking at a traffic light for the first time. Their minds are engaged with the traffic lights. Similarly, when your child is at home, he or she could be thinking about something else. It could be the teddy or toys; it could be the smell of good food, or it could even be that they simply want to go out. Once they become fixated on an idea, they don't like to lose control over it.

That is why you should never be upset or frustrated with them when you notice their behavior. In fact, that is something to be happy about. I might imagine you are surprised right now. Why should parents be happy that their children are stubborn over some things? We all know that children are not able to clearly rationalize things. But when they become stubborn about something, it is their way of analyzing it and figuring it out. That shows emotional maturity and that is a good thing.

Make sure that you also check that your child is not facing any other problem. I once knew a mother who would often become frustrated because his or her daughter would act up and often throw tantrums whenever they were told to do something. Her mother tried everything – even being a little stern – but her daughter would only show more resistance. In the end, it turns out that the girl's second molars were growing and the process was rather painful. The girl could obviously not focus on anything beyond the pain and he or she didn't know how to handle things. Children don't plan. They merely react. Even when they laugh at the expense of your pain, they do so because their empathy has not been developed enough to understand what you are going through, which is why it comes down to you to explain to them and help them understand.

## To Sit or Stand

One of the more common doubts that parents seem to have about potty training is figuring out whether they should have their son stand up or sit down while peeing. Many articles, videos, and experts say that you should have your son sit down while others say that standing up helps him learn to quickly pee when he has to.

I think that it is about personal choice. Teach your child what you think is best. You can do one of two things:

- You can teach your child to pee while standing and later, encourage them to pee when they are sitting on the potty to poop. This helps because if you can help them pee while standing, then you have technically trained them in one aspect – which is peeing – and now you only have to worry about teaching them to poop properly.

- On the other hand, you can teach them to pee and poop while sitting down, helping them to take their time to use the potty. This may be a slower process but it helps your child to properly finish what he wants to do.

In the end, do what you think will help your child progress? You know him best. Think about how he likes to learn things, what he is usually curious about, what instructions he finds easy to understand, and other important factors. They can help you decide how you would like to help your child learn.

Here's an example. I know a mother whose son would stand up and watch kid's videos on YouTube. He or she simply enjoyed staying on his feet. That gave his or her mother an idea. He or she decided to teach him or her to pee while standing. Lo and behold. The idea worked. He or she would even make him or her watch a video as she prepared him or her to pee, then close the mobile phone, and let him know that he could continue watching once he finished peeing. He or she would do this gently, without appearing upset or frustrated. It took a while for her son or daughter to grasp the idea, but eventually, he or she was peeing all by himself or herself.

# CHAPTER 4:

## Celebrations and Rewards

Everyone says that everything we say to a child will become their inner dialogue. If we always tell them, "no, you can't, you never do," that is what they are going to hear all day long. When you are potty training, the words change just a bit, too, "pee goes in the potty, not on the floor." It isn't surprising that some toddlers will end up shutting down. They will just quit listening to you. There is when you will see them not take one more step to learn their new skill. They have mentally thrown in the towel and have told themselves that they just can't do it. Those words won't ever spark any confidence in any child.

Yes, you have to set boundaries when you are potty training your child, and yes, you are right; pee doesn't belong on the floor.

What most parents overlook is the very important role of praise. When you do praise right, it can help you and your child on their potty training journey. If it is done wrong, it can make things a lot messier.

Praise is the most important tool that many parents overlook when trying to get their child potty trained. There is why you must celebrate the smallest wins when you are potty training your child.

Potty training is exhausting. You have to understand that first of all. At the same time, you can try your best to change up your schedule so you can be home for three days to get your child potty trained. Life does continue while you potty train.

All your normal life happenings are still going to need your attention. So, it is extremely easy for any parent, even the ones with the best intentions, to end up with tunnel vision when potty training.

You might even miss seeing the progress your child has made because you stay focused on all their mistakes. After you have been potty training for a few days, anybody wants it to be over. You have to remember that with any other milestone in your child's life, did they learn it overnight? Did they wake up one morning and just start walking? Just because your child didn't pick up potty training in three days doesn't mean that something is wrong with them.

Think about all the things that your child has to learn in just a few days:

- They have to feel pee

- They have to get to the potty

- They have to push down their pants

- They have to get onto the potty

- They have to release their poop or pee

- They have to wipe

- They have to flush

- They have to wash their hands

Now, they have to learn all these steps and in the correct order. There is something that they didn't have to know just a few days earlier. It is all new to them.

Now, reflect on what they are going through when they get something wrong. Learning new things can be messy, right? Everyone makes mistakes when they are learning new things. It is all part of the process.

How are you obtainable to feel if the person trying to teach you is only noticing your mistakes? You aren't going to feel too good about yourself, are you? Now put yourself in your toddler's shoes. If you are putting your toddler in their kind of environment, things just aren't going to click, are they? Is there a language that could help you with their process?

Praise. You have to praise your child for the things that they do right. If you only focus on what they do wrong, your child might start thinking: "Nope, can't do the potty."

Your child needs to know that it is fine to make mistakes. If your child is still having accidents on the fifth day and you are still saying: "NO! Pee goes in the potty!!!" then you are missing out on all the small victories. What are the small victories? The small victories might be that your child realized they were peeing for felt the pee but didn't get to the potty fast enough. Show them the small wins and remind them what they should do the following time. "Hey, honey, you knew you needed to pee, but you just didn't make it to the potty on time. Then let's try to get there faster."

By saying something like there, you are your child's team member, and you are building up their confidence. Pride is a child's biggest motivator when potty training. When you can do it there, it doesn't become a battle between you and your child, but you and your child fight against pee and poop. When your child makes it to the bathroom, give them a high five, sticker, and whatever you can reward them with. Your child has to be rewarded when they do something right.

You have to remember that potty training is a process, and it isn't going to click in one moment. If your child isn't picking up potty training in only a few days, it doesn't mean that they won't ever. There are things you can act to help them along

- Check yourself… are you sharing bad vibes and your frustration with your child?

- A good night's sleep can reset everyone. Try to acquire as much rest as your child does.

- Celebrate all the small wins.

The easiest way to potty train is to remain focused on each moment and not where you would like to be tomorrow or where you were yesterday. Remember to watch your language around your child. You need to use language to give your child confidence boosts to let them know that they can rock potty training.

## Celebration Ideas

If you notice that bribing is working to keep your child motivated, here are some ideas you can use.

- Make a big show of them becoming a "big kid." If your toddler is still sleeping in a crib, they reward them with a "big kid" bed once they are trained. There would be an enormous time to transition them into a real bed. Big kids use the potty, so big kids get to sleep in real beds. There is a great way to switch their frame of mind.

- If your family loves to twirl like mine does, with every successful use of the potty, allow the child and their siblings to have a dance party for a few minutes after. Put some music on and cheer, dance, and clap for the new big kid. They will love all the attention and fun family time.

- Games… there are potty training games on the internet. Allow your little one to play one for a predetermined amount of time with every successful use of the potty. Some websites have ideas for games you can play while training your child to use the potty.

- Charts… sticker charts are a great way for your child to track how well they are doing. They catch to put a sticker on the chart for each time they successfully use the potty; everybody can see their progress and get to celebrate with them.

- Potty prizes… are fun ways to show your encouragement and support. They are also a fun bribe. Whatever your child loves, find several things you can put into a plastic container. My child loved stickers, fruit snacks, movies, paw patrol, and lots more I could list but don't have the time or space. When they used the potty, they got to pick out a prize from the container. They loved their special present. Once they were able to poop in the potty, they got a larger prize. When going to the potty became a normal routine, the smaller prizes were enough to keep them encourages. Continue giving the potty prizes until there aren't any more accidents throughout the day. You can still expect a slip up now and then, but they will soon be using the potty like a pro.

- Fun underwear… take your child shopping and permit them to pick out their special underwear. Putting on a pair of underwear with their favorite character on them will motivate them not to mess them up. I recommend using pull up at nap time and bedtime.

## Throwing a Potty Training Party

Having a potty training party is a great way to kick off your child's potty training journey. You could throw another one after they have been successfully potty trained. Gather family and friends around to celebrate another milestone in your child's life.

Let's talk about the party set up. What is a party without decorations, good ambiance, and great food? Whatever your child's favorite colors are, that's what you should go for. If your son wants pink and purple, you use pink and purple. The food needs to be simple finger foods like pizza, cupcakes, chips, juice, crackers, etc. Any child-friendly will work.

I asked some of the moms who had successfully potty trained a child or two attending to write out phrases that they used when they were potty training their children. These are the ones I liked the best: "Love. Love. Love." "Follow Daddy." "All about the bribes." "Flushing fun." "You did it!"

### Hosting a Potty Party

Hosting a potty party is super easy. You might be trying to get your toddle excited about learning to use the potty, or you are celebrating huge success. A potty party adds excitement and fun to their potty training experience.

### Invitations

The first thing you demand to do is to invite your family and friends. Invite all the children you know who have recently been or are getting ready to be trained and be prepared to have loads of fun.

### Games

A party isn't a party without games. Throw those dirty diapers always with a game of "diaper toss." The children take turns throwing diapers into a trash can. When they toss a diaper, they can tell those nasty goodbyes while saying hello to the big kid pants.

Another game is to have everyone bring a potty seat and play a game of "can do it." It is like "duck, duck, goose, but the kids will go around the circle saying, "I can, I can, I can do it."

### Sweet Treats

A party isn't complete without something sweet. Every child who has learned how to use the potty wants some treats to help them celebrate their wins.

### Have Fun

Allow your child to help you plan their party. After all, it is all about them. If their favorite thing is Teenage Mutant Ninja Turtles, then have all the decorations about Teenage Mutant Ninja Turtles. Let them pick out their favorite music, songs, etc. If they are artistic and want to have a paint party, have a paint party. Set up a table covered with paper, markers, paints, etc. Just remember to make everything water washable.

# Common Mistakes

## Inconsistency

Toddlers tend to do better when they know exactly what to expect. They become more resilient and agreeable based on how consistent you are and how predictable the situations. The tendency of being inconsistent is you send mixed signals to your children which could be confusing for them.

Keep regular routines and schedules. Keeping a diary and taking notes might help to keep things consistent as well.

## Try Not to Begin Too Soon

Whether Nancy down the road began toilet preparing when she was 2 doesn't imply that your child will be prepared at 2. Children develop at different rates, both rationally and physically - and toilet preparing is both mental and physical. Give your child a chance to develop and develop at his own rate.

## Try Not to Be Negative

Positive reinforcement goes a lot more remote than negative castigating. If your child has an accident, don't have a fit, or more awful, upbraid the child for coming up short. Simply utilize a "we'll improve next time" approach and make sure to adulate your child when they accomplish something right.

## Try Not to Surge Preparing Your Child

Pretty much any article you see that discussions about potty preparing tips will reveal that you can't surge these things. Hurrying toilet preparing or going at a faster pace than what your child is alright with is just going to baffle both of you and cause a great deal of anxiety in your child. Give your child a chance to lead the movement.

## Try Not to Worry

When you get focused on, your child gets pushed. You don't need any anxiety or negative feelings coordinated at any part of the toilet preparing process. Try not to wrinkle your nose or state negative things. You don't need your child to connect anything negative with this experience. If you need success in toilet preparing children, remain quiet and perky.

**Try Not to Be Caught Ill-Equipped**

You can't close yourself and your child in your home until your child is prepared to go to the toilet, which is unreasonable – and probably undesirable. You should go to the store, church, out to supper and different trips so to maintain a strategic distance from any issues, simply ensure you are readied. Bring wipes, a change of clothes, and plastic bags for ruined clothes and you might need to think about a versatile potty. Toddlers usually aren't exceptionally fond of sitting on strange toilets.

**Going Overboard with Family Time**

Most children value one-on-one time with their parents. This creates deeper bonding and avoids the pitfalls of rivalry between siblings to keep your attention. Getting the family involved in potty training is okay but too much involvement may not be beneficial.

Try to reserve a certain amount of time for just you and your potty training child. This will make him or her trust you and the process of training.

## Scolding and Punishment

After receiving a punishment, your child naturally becomes fearful. Whether the fear lasts for a few seconds or a lifetime, this is something that impacts your child's ability to learn. When fear takes over the brain, it becomes the main focus. Even if your child knows exactly what needs to be done, they might begin to second-guess themselves after being punished for not using the bathroom (or for having an accident). In this way, scolding or punishing your child can backfire when it comes to the progress that you have made. It can be challenging to get your child to a place where they no longer feel this fear.

Aside from developing a fear of using the bathroom, punishing your child for these reasons can also strain your relationship. While punishment is a necessary disciplinary action, sometimes they cause more damages than helping a parent when it comes to potty training. Because you will be continually helping your child use the bathroom, you need to have a trusting relationship in the process. Even if the punishment isn't long-lasting, its impact might be. Children choose to hold on to certain things that you might not even realize they are holding on to. Along with halting any potty training progress, this can also cause your child to become fearful of future new situations.

Overall, it just makes sense to skip out on the punishment when you are potty training your child. While it can be an incredibly frustrating job for both of you, remember that each child will eventually develop the skills. It is a natural instinct that needs time to develop. When you punish your child for not learning this fast enough, it causes them to feel humiliated. Imaginably, this can also impact your child's future learning abilities. They will likely want to give up if they don't get it right the first time to fear being scolded or punished.

A distressed child is one who is more likely to have accidents. This is another way that punishment can backfire while you are potty training. It becomes a never-ending cycle of showing your disappointment and your child feeling intimidated by it. The trick is to let your child know that potty training is possible for all people and ages. By sending a message that it is only a "big girl" responsibility, you can also place the wrong kind of pressure on them. Take away all of the intimidating aspects that you can. This will help your child feel as though they can accomplish it on their own.

By avoiding punishment, you are taking all of the stress out of the process of potty training. Many parents don't realize this until it is too late and they have already tried using punishments. A stress-free environment is not only a great thing for potty training but also for the entire household. When you are holding on to that type of tension, it can easily become contagious. Even if you are trying to hide it, your child will likely sense it from you.

If you find it difficult to potty train without punishment, you need to make sure that your mood and feelings are checked. Do not try to work with your child if you are in a bad mood, regardless of what is causing you stress. You will be more likely to snap or punish your child, and this will only send the wrong messages, as you know. Try to remain in the most uplifted mood that you can each time that you begin potty training. The experience is supposed to be fun and exciting, so you must have a demeanor to match.

Another option is to teach the child to get out of the bed and wake up a parent to use the bathroom at night. Of course, this means that you will continually have to get up and help your child throughout the night, but it could be a quick way to teach them that they can use the bathroom if necessary, to avoid wetting the bed. When you choose to go with this method, your child will likely pick up on the idea quickly. This means that you should only have to remain on-call for a short period until they feel comfortable. Ensure that the bathroom is well lit by nightlights and that any potty chair or other device is set up and ready to use. This will make your child's experience one that seems more suitable to tackle alone.

I recommend using pull-ups frequently when your child needs to go for an extended period without using the bathroom. This can be a good solution for when you are in the car and do not have the option to stop. Your child will likely be eating and drinking in the car, and this means that they are highly likely to need to use the bathroom. If you feel that they won't be able to hold it during the whole duration of the car ride, then opting for pull-ups is a smart move in this case. You must play it by ear as to what you feel your child is ready for.

I wish you the best of luck for an exciting and enjoyable period of potty training. You will also want to keep in mind that your ultimate goal for your child is about more than just potty training. It is about helping your child learn, grow, and adapt to the world we live in. Potty training is just one more milestone, one more task to master, and your child will be so proud to say "I go potty."

# CHAPTER 6:

## What Is Positive Discipline

Wikipedia describes Positive Discipline as a type of discipline model that focuses on the child's positive behavior.

It is based on the concept that there are no bad children, only bad behaviors. Other related teachings include:

- Good behaviors can be taught and reinforced. Bad behaviors can be corrected and modified without hurting them physically or emotionally.

- Verbal punishment is sometimes more damaging than physical punishment, leaving children insecure, anxious, or fearful.

Positive Discipline aims to promote family togetherness, cooperation, and treating each other with respect. It is geared to encouraging parents to train their children in making good choices, solve problems, and make agreements that foster creativity and critical thinking. It does not rely on punishments or rewards. Instead, it utilizes the power of empathy, active listening, relationship building, and mutual respect to develop positive behaviors.

**It is focused on:**

- Non-punitive solutions

- Respectful and non-violent interactions

- Identifying the meaning behind the behavior

- Effective and clear communication

- Building self-esteem and capability

- Encouragement (instead of praise)

- Connection and Play

- Finding long-term solutions to develop self-discipline

- Mutually respectful parent and child relationship

- Teaching lifelong skills

- Increases confidence and competence to handle difficult situations

This approach is not new. It became popular in the 1920s when psychologists Dr. Alfred Adler and Dr. Rudolf Dreikurs introduced the idea of positive discipline to the audiences in the United States. Dr. Adler focused his attention on parenting education, actively teaching parents to treat their children with respect. He also argued that pampering and spoiling children could result in behavioral and social problems. Thus, he advocated against them. The classroom management techniques were initially introduced during the same period in Vienna, Austria. However, it was only in the late 1930s that Dr. Dreikurs brought it to the U.S.

Their advocacy became the basis of Positive Discipline, an approach that is designed and developed by Dr. Jane Nelsen to help parents, mentors, and other authorities raise responsible, resilient, and independent children. It teaches essential life and social skills in a manner or approach that maintains mutual respect and encourages a deeper understanding of the discipline.

To make Positive Discipline more effective, it is necessary for parents, teachers, and other adult influences to create a nurturing environment that meets all the basic needs of the child, such as food, shelter, and clothing, extending to non-physical needs such as love, encouragement, and acceptance.

- Parental love is about the unconditional love that is acted out by providing care and gentle guidance, giving time and attention to children, and resolving any social conflict.
- Acceptance makes children feel that no matter what they do, whether wrong or right, they are loved.
- Encouragement is showing support in concrete ways that help children figure out how to avoid or correct mistakes, including finding their strengths to pursue passions and life goals.

In a nutshell, parents are the primary support of children who ensure their positive growth and development.

**Positive Discipline at Home**

Discipline begins at home. As early as possible, kids are taught to be responsible for their actions and distinguish right from wrong. Positive Discipline at home uses healthy and positive interactions to prevent inappropriate acts or behavioral problems before they begin and become habits. It teaches kids the correct behavior and be respectful through appreciation, encouragement, consequences, and other non-violent strategies.

The outcomes are:

- Children do better when there is routine, consistency, and lots of positive encouragement.
- A positive relationship with parents dramatically reduces the occurrence of challenging behavior.
- A non-punitive discipline that provides significant long-term benefits compared to punishment.
- Children respond positively to parents or caregivers whom they trust. It is essential to use the strategies consistently by all caregivers.

1.  Creating a safe environment

Childproof your home and supervise his movements to see that he is safe while exploring his immediate surroundings.

2.  Establishing a routine

Routines help children perform or behave appropriately because they know the expectations of their parents. A specific way to guarantee optimum care, safety, and enjoyment will help your child feel secure, more in control, and less anxious, hence developing strong self-discipline.

3.  Planning ahead

If you have to run errands and need to take your child with you, it is necessary to talk to him and let him know your expectations of his behaviors. It will prepare him and try his best to behave well. However, for little children who do not fully comprehend yet what you are trying to say, better have toys, crayons, books, and other activity tools with you when you go out to keep them occupied while shopping, waiting for the doctor's appointment, or traveling.

4.   Having clear expectations

Discuss your expectation with your child. If you set 5 expectations like—Be Kind, Be Respectful, Be Responsible, Be Helpful, and Be Safe, do not forget to tell them. Have a conversation with him about the acts and deeds that demonstrate your expectations. Make sure that you also display those acceptable behaviors because your child is always watching your examples.

5.   Offering choices

Choices that are suitable for his age will help him gain a sense of independence and self-control. By offering options, you empower him to become more decisive and stand up for what he believes is right for him. It also applies to the consequences of misbehavior or disobeying your rules. Make him choose between two safe, logical values that aim to give him a lesson and a warning not to repeat the mistake. Always follow through and enforce the consequence to make him see that you are serious about Discipline.

6.   Building a positive relationship

Spending quality time with your child reinforces your relationship, helping him develop a strong sense of belonging, significance, and connection. Allow him to choose the activity or topic. It also lessens the occurrence of misbehavior because he does not want to disappoint you.

7.  Redirecting the negative behavior

Maybe your child is bored, or for whatever reason, he starts acting out. It is essential to provide a suitable alternative that will stop him from misbehaving and enjoy himself. Always see to it that your child is well-rested, well-fed, and engaged in stimulating and fun activities. Redirecting his sudden malicious behavior to another activity that interests him will generate appropriate action.

8.  Calm down before you address misbehavior

Do not try to discipline your child when you are angry, frustrated, or experiencing physical or mental fatigue because you will lose your objectivity. Calm yourself first and take a time out to steady your nerves. It will help you think clearly and handle the situation somewhat yet firmly.

9.  Being firm and kind at the same time

It is the Positive Discipline in its best form. You respond to each situation or misbehavior with kindness and respect to your child, but firm enough to impose the consequences. It is also essential to let your child explain and justify his acts, but no matter how convincing his reason, make him understand that rules are rules.

Remind him that you set limits for a purpose—to keep him safe and prevent mistakes that may hurt him or others. If he chooses to defy any of them, he needs to face the consequences of his actions.

10. Catch him being good

Do not let good deeds go unnoticed. Whenever you observe your child behaving properly, appreciate his efforts, so he is aware that he is doing well.

## Distinguishing Factors between Normal Behavior and Misbehavior

What makes you think that your child is displaying misbehavior or expected behavior? It is necessary to have truthful expectations about your kid's behavior, considering the stage of his development. Every step has distinct challenges that trigger actions, which you can mistakenly view as intentional misbehavior. By understanding these stages, you will know the difference.

Here are some examples of typical or developmentally appropriate behavior:

Example No. 1:

- Developmentally Appropriate or Normal Behavior: Tantrums
- Developmental Tasks: The child is beginning to handle his frustrations and throws tantrums when upset and does not understand why he needs to do something. A classic example is when he does not want to brush his teeth or go to bed early.

Example No. 2:

- Developmentally Appropriate or Normal Behavior: Energetic and Active
- Developmental Tasks: The need to explore and discover. One manifestation is the difficulty of sitting quietly for a long time, like during church attendance or storytelling period.

Example No. 3:

- Developmentally Appropriate or Normal Behavior: Independent
- Developmental Tasks: He wants to do things on his own like feeding himself, choosing clothes to wear, or picking the toys he wants to play with.

Example No. 4:

- Developmentally Appropriate or Normal Behavior: Being talkative
- Developmental Tasks: He becomes curious about everything around him, so he asks many questions. His vocabulary is also growing, so he is excited to use the words he learns.

When your child is misbehaving:


- Halt whatever you are doing and give your full attention to your child.
- Remain calm and speak with your normal voice tone.
- If out in a public area, remove him from the situation that triggers his emotional outburst.
- Get down to his eye level.
- Make him understand what you feel before reminding your child about your expectations from him. "I know that you still want to play, but it is time to go home."
- Discuss the expected behavior and asks him what he needs to do about it.
- State the consequence of the misbehavior.
- Follow through with the consequence.
- Acknowledge when you see your child correcting his behavior.
- Reconnect and restore your relationship through affection, hugs, or plays.

Dealing with a little child can be tiring and challenging, so do not forget to take care of yourself. It is a must to find time for yourself and find support when necessary.

- Eat a healthy diet and exercise regularly.
- Spend time in nature or have a "me" time to relax.
- Engage in activities that make you feel good and happy. Do them regularly.
- Keep in touch with family and friends.
- Say no to extra responsibilities.

# CHAPTER 7:

## The Objective of Discipline

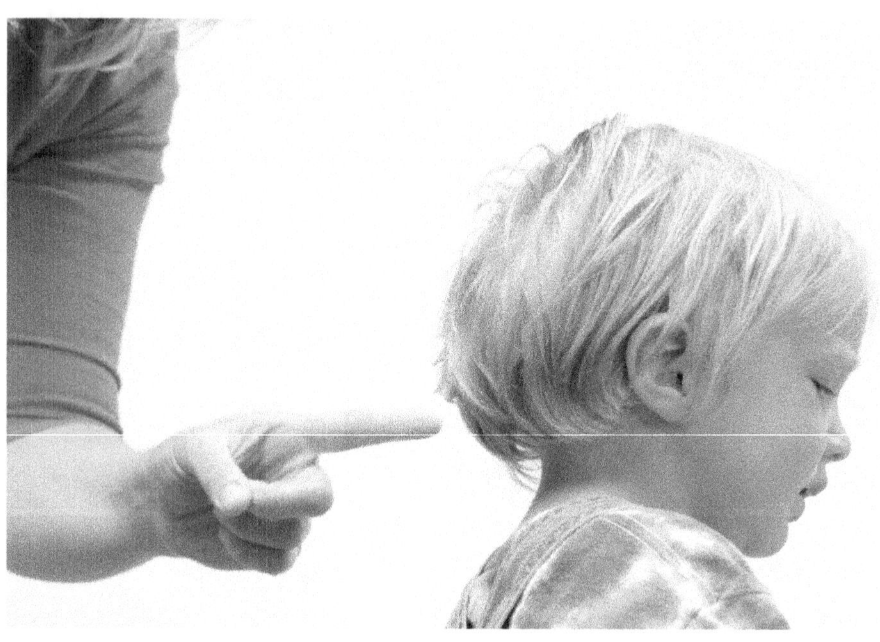

The objective of disciplining your child is not to punish, but to improve the child and help them act like they are supposed to. Since child discipline, at times, is indeed one of the least fanciful aspects of parenting, the challenge that comes with it might make you want to think that it is impossible to discipline your child without punishing them.

The truth is, resorting to punishment is not an excellent way to teach a lesson to your kids. You might interview some parents, and you want to confirm what pattern of discipline they use. You might hear them say: "I use them, interchangeably." But the proper question is, are those words synonyms? Obviously no!

But why is it that the objectives of disciplining are never to punish? When a parent punishes a child, the child would undoubtedly be affected physically. Moreover, in most cases, the brain is involved. All parents would desire a healthy mind for their kids.

Additionally, punishment is fear-based. And consistent fear is not healthy for the brain. But sadly, many parents hope that threatening as part of a sentence will instill fear, and fear, in turn, will discard that undesired behavior and pick up a desired one.

Little wonder that they didn't realize that they are unknowingly messing up their kid's brain. It is capable of mental disorder, stress hormone elevation, emotion dysregulation, and externalizing behavior. In some cases, they become bullies or victims. In sharp contrast to punishment, discipline improves a child's well-being. It allows a child to focus on the right lesson; they avoid being vindictive, distrustful, and spiteful.

Positive discipline is one of the beautiful examples of a zero-punishment disciplinary strategy that is dependent on mutual respect and positive instruction. It breeds learning culture rather than focusing on punishing. It adopts the use of encouraging words and a tool to motivate them constructively. But how can this be implemented? I'll show you in an example. It should teach you how positive discipline works.

I want to assume that your child often delays your morning routine. Each morning, you have to wrestle with the same struggle. And what exactly does he do? He plays while brushing his teeth, and he ends up spending a lot of time, in fact, more than 20 minutes, and this delays you. How do you correct this and not resolve to punishment?

You have to identify the underlying issue. Could it be that not getting enough time to play in the morning and brushing teeth offers that privilege? What exactly are you doing wrong? Could you hurry him up to wake up, go potty, eat breakfast, put clothes on, and brush his teeth? From here, did you sense that there's no room for her to play? Honestly, the routine is boring.

So, you have to address the problem. And how can you do that using this scenario, you can wake up 10-15 minutes ahead of time, rather than the usual time of waking up? The excess time gives him the ability to obtain the free rein to play, and yes, there would not be a need to rush her. And after that, you can let her focus on preparing for school.

After this stage, you have a task left to accomplish, which is, teaching him the natural consequences. And to get that work, you should tell him that you can't risk getting late. So, if the opportunity to play granted and time to prepare for the school set, there is not going to be a retreat.

If it is time, you will go no matter what. Even if they haven't changed pajamas or brushing teeth, you will have to go! And do not forget to be firm with that limit. Don't you think he'll learn better? Definitely, and that's the natural consequence.

Well, while you do this, cap it all with encouraging words. So, they get things right on time, praise them. And before you know it, they have already learned that and put it into the routine. And yes, you did not punish, all you applied was just natural consequences.

Discipline should be given by someone that has a bond with the child. When they simply are told to behave by authority figures, they might not respond as well, so do not always wait for others to discipline them. You are in charge of their behavior. If others agree that you are too lenient or too strict, that is on them. Focus only on the best methods for both you and your child.

It needs to be consistent and shouldn't be something that confuses children. They'll start to question why it is OK for some kids to do one thing while they get punished for the same, especially if those other kids are their friends, cousins, and siblings. They will also be confused about why it is OK for them to scream and yell outside with no shoes on when you are in a good mood, but why you snap when you are in a bad mood. If something is terrible behavior, address it no matter the situation. If it is decent behavior, be cautious before punishing strictly.

It has to be fair treatment and something that the child can understand as appropriate as well. While they might do something more hurtful to you than even your closest friend would, you can't punish them in the same way you might towards an adult. It must do in a way that they can understand and see the natural consequences.

Discipline needs to base on the developmental stage of the child. You would not discipline your six-year-old the same way that you would your two-year-old. Ensure that no children get special treatment and make it completely clear how discipline differs based on their age if they question fairness.

Discipline should also aim to be something that can help the child grow, nothing that is going to hold them back (Effective, 2004).

## Natural Consequences

The best kind of discipline is when a child can see the natural consequences of their actions. By definition, natural effects are the direct and unpleasant result of a child's activity. When a child makes terrible choices, and a parent allows them to go through the natural consequences, they helped to correct their behavior. They learn to adjust themselves, and they are compelled or willing to seek a more desired outcome.

As earlier emphasized, natural consequences are sure the best way to discipline children. For one thing, natural values are not established by parents as against punishment that could sap your strength; instead, they are the results of a child's choices or actions. As a result of this, the child would admit that the effect they have is the outcome of their inappropriate behavior. With this pattern, they admit faults and would swiftly take to corrections without feeling any resentment.

But as you see, you might hurriedly think that natural consequences are simple to figure out. It is not always the case. If you struggle to see the sound effects for your life, then your toddler will as well. Always be aware and cautious of the cause and reaction of words and behaviors.

What's essential about helping your child see the natural consequences is refraining from using the terms like "I told you so," and things that will belittle or shame them. When you do that, it becomes a competition, and they will take it upon themselves to, in return, prove you wrong. It can happen as early as childhood to the times that they are teenagers.

Let's look at a typical example—the candy debate. Your child is consistent in asking for more, and more, and more. You are pretty sure that if they do not stop soon, they're going to feel sick, but their asking is relentless. Tell them, "You can have as much candy as you want, but too much is going to make you feel sick."

They might think you are right and ignore their wishes for more. Most children will not care and take this as a chance to do whatever they want. Later on, in the night, you might see that they are feeling sick and holding their stomach. They will ask you what's wrong with them, and you might feel the urge to say something like, "I warned you that if you did not stop, you would feel sick."

Instead of using this language with them, try to be empathetic. Tell that you have been through a scenario like this, you know what it feels like want too much candy. If you are always overeating, eventually, eating candy is not fun anymore. They might not listen this first time either, but you are setting them up so that they know that they will be able to decide whether or not they want more candy. Of course, do not let them eat as much candy as they want. It would just be for things like birthday parties or Halloween when candy is surrounding them.

Furthermore, when implementing natural consequences, always allow your child to know what exactly you will not be doing for them anymore. In this situation, you put control in their hands. It is up to them now to decide what amount of candy is suitable for them. It will help them to be more responsible and aware of how their actions can have natural consequences. Always follow through, do not create a premise for shame, and ensure that consistency is favorably upheld. Of course, do your best to prevent the child from serious harm.

Maybe your child is continually unbuckling their seatbelt in the car, always wanting to run around. You do not want to drive like a maniac to try and prove them wrong. You do not want to slam on your brakes and send them flying through the car. Instead, pull over on the side of the road. Sit there and tell them that you can't drive unless they put their seatbelt on. They will eventually get bored and understand that they need to wear their belt if they want to be able to go to the next fun destination you are on your way to.

Do not forget, natural consequences create a premise where you are not to blame; instead, your child will. Even though in some situations, natural effects might not be feasible because at times we would unconsciously be involved in the process. Interestingly natural results still prove to be the best way to teach a child since it will allow your child to make choices that lead to good outcomes that will positively impact everyone.

So, allowing them to go through their negative outcome, they tend to understand the importance of self-correction.

In cases where you'd not want to use natural consequences, use logical consequences to deprive them of some privileges. Teach—in extreme cases, confidently teach lessons. Allow them to write—sure you'd have taught them that fighting is wrong, instead of being on repeat mode, have them write about why the fight is wrong and how they will avoid it in the future.

We could still go further to understand some common occurrences in parenting. Take, for example, many parents spank their child, and just for a simple cry, they discipline them—not punish. Is that approach a clever one?

# CHAPTER 8:

## The Positive Approach and Basic Concept

Parents are the biggest influences in the life of their children's development, growth, success, and happiness. As they grow older, more people come into their sphere of existence, casting various types of influence.

Parenting becomes more challenging nowadays because of the advent of modern technology, which provides easy ways to share the child's accomplishments and milestones on social media. Somehow, it makes parenting a competitive sport. But, regardless of your parenting style and strategies, the fact remains that it is your job to prepare your child for his life journey and provide him with the essential needs—structure, support, safety, and love.

## Why the Positive Approach?

In contrast to the negative disciplinary approach that involves punishment in different forms, positive discipline encourages positive behaviors and decision-making. It is based on the concept that you can teach and reinforce good behavior without hurting your child physically or verbally. It teaches parents and mentors to be firm and kind at the same time. In short, positive discipline is neither permissive nor punitive.

In this approach, you are not ignoring the issues about your child's behavior. You are actively helping him handle the situations in the best way possible, without losing your temper. You remain friendly, respectful, and calm as you teach him to become more responsible and accountable for his behavior.

The positive approach allows you to use different reinforcement and consequence options after establishing rules and reasonable limits. This encourages your child to stay within limits and be responsible. In case he goes beyond the limit or defies the rules, he knows that he needs to remedy the situation to avoid the consequences. Moreover, positive discipline allows you to teach your child to practice acceptable behaviors in a kind, yet firm approach. This method helps you communicate clearly with him what behaviors are appropriate and what are inappropriate. It does not use advocate spanking, yelling, or severe punishment, it focuses on problem-solving and encouragement.

## Why Teaching Positive Discipline is Vital?

- It teaches a strong sense of responsibility, problem-solving skills, self-discipline, and cooperation.

- It helps children manage their emotions.

- It builds and strengthens self-esteem.

- It fosters mutual respect and trust.

- It invites children to develop their brand of significance, letting them contribute in ways that bring meaning and fulfillment.

- It forms new connections in your child's brain, which promotes better relationships.

- It guides children to handle stress in a positive and healthy way.

- It provides a more in-depth understanding that there are certain people that influence or has power to what happens in their life.

To further understand this method of discipline, you need to explore its salient points.

## A. Criteria for Positive Discipline

*1. It Is Both Firm and Kind.* It promotes mutual encouragement and respect that strengthens the parent-child relationship during the teaching process. Children learn good habits by imitating their parents and other role models around them. Teaching, by example, is the best way to instill discipline.

- Be respectful and kind, even if you are upset.

- Refrain from yelling, humiliating, or calling him names to prevent him from copying you when he becomes upset over something in the future. Seeing you calm and composed while dealing with the situation teaches him that this strategy is better compared to panicking or getting mad.

Aside from that, kindness encourages your child to become more receptive to reasoning, calm down, and cooperate. However, it is important to remember that kindness in this context is not synonymous with giving in or permissiveness. You are still teaching him self-discipline, in a kind way and firm way. You say NO, but in a tone that is not mean or harsh.

Furthermore, you expect him to follow the limits you set and enforce consequences when he acts otherwise. This method helps your child practice cognitive thinking, helping him master skills that he will need to make more complex decision-making in the future.

*2. It Promotes a Sense of Belonging and Significance.* Positive discipline promotes a sense of connection, eliminating deep-seated fear of being punished or grounded. It can be demonstrated by communicating your discipline plan or rules, then explaining the consequences that you will enforce if he disobeys or misbehaves.

If you are introducing a new rule or discipline technique, discuss it with your child so he will know how to adjust. It should not come out of the blue. In this way, you are showing him that you are working together during the learning process. It will make him feel significant and more compliant to conform to the new rule, limit, or consequence.

It works well with older children who already understand the science and reasoning behind the discipline. Kids below the age of three find it quite difficult to understand the consequences or make a sound judgment because the prefrontal cortex of the brain is not yet developed. For this age group, redirection strategies should be used. Parents should understand age-related behaviors and enforce appropriate discipline techniques.

*3. It Teaches Essential Life and Social Skills.* Positive discipline is geared toward the development of skills, problem-solving, cooperation, respect, and concern for others. All these factors are important factors for the child's development and ability to contribute to the larger community, school, and home.

*4. It Leads to the Discovery of Personal Power.* This kind of discipline invites children to discover that they are capable of doing great things. They learn it when they obey and do positive deeds, or when they receive an appreciation, praise, acceptance, or a reward.

*5. Its Effectiveness Is Long-Term.* Positive discipline prepares your child for adulthood. What he is learning now will effectively help him thrive and survive in the future.

# B. The Core of Positive Discipline

To fully comprehend the rationale of Positive Discipline, it is important to understand its context as an approach to instill child discipline. It originates from "disciplina," the Latin word which means teaching and comes from another term "discipulus" or pupil. It is about teaching and providing vital learning that the pupil can use in his lifetime. But over the years, discipline becomes synonymous with punishing and not teaching.

Thanks to Dr. Alfred Adler and Dr. Rudolf Dreikurs, who advocated that children be treated with respect by adults. Their ideas were later picked up by child psychologists, advocates, and authors who want to spread awareness that punishment is not the best method to fix the behavior of children or resolve problems. One of them is Dr. Jane Nelsen. She conceptualized Positive Discipline based on the teachings of these brilliant men. In 1981, she wrote and self-published the Positive Discipline book, which was picked up by Ballantine Books (now a Random House subsidiary) and published the succeeding editions including the books which she co-authored.

*1. There Is No Such Thing as Bad Kids, Only Bad Behavior*

At the core of Positive Discipline is the general statement that "there is no such thing as bad children, only bad behavior." It is important for parents to bear in mind that kids are naturally good and they have episodes of acting up due to certain reasons that they cannot voice out, especially when they are young and do not know how to process their emotions.

There are two factors behind the challenging behavior of your child—the sense of not belonging (connection) and the sense of significance (contribution). When one or both of these basic needs are not satisfied, the children find a way to fulfill it, even if it requires negative action. Dr. Dreikurs aptly put it by stating that "A misbehaving child is a discouraged child."

Calling the child "bad" for doing something negative is not healthy for his self-esteem. It usually starts when your kid continually misbehaves or throw tantrums, and you are exasperated. While trying to calm him, you slip and label him as a "bad boy" unintentionally. You can forgive yourself after that slip and quote the famous cliché that you are just human and commit mistakes, but if you keep repeating it every time, he does something wrong, it will be engraved in his mind and damage his self-worth.

Positive Discipline aims to help parents learn to objectify the behavior and cut the "bad cycle." For example, instead of telling your child when he hits his younger sibling that "that's bad" or "you're such a bad boy," you may say "it is not okay to hit your brother when you are angry because he does not share his toy" and then let him understand the harm that might happen to his brother. When you objectify his behavior, you are teaching him the cause and effect. By directly addressing the "bad behavior" without using the term "bad," you are encouraging your child to make better choices and avoid hurting other people.

*2. Show the Child How to Resolve the Problem, Instead of Pointing Out That What He Did Is Wrong*

Redirecting the behavior of your child requires more than saying "Don't do that" or "No." It needs skills to teach him right from wrong using calm actions and words. For instance, you catch your child before he can hit his little brother, instead of saying "No hitting" or "Don't hit," tell him to "Ask his brother nicely if he wants to borrow a toy." By giving him an alternative way to get the toy, you are showing him that asking is more effective than hitting.

If he already hit his brother, it is a must to be creative with your response. One good way is enforcing a non-punitive time-out, which technically is about removing the child from the stimulus that triggers his behavior and allows him to calm down. You can cuddle him when he is very upset, let him play in his room, or ask him to sit with you and read a book. After his emotion subsides, start explaining (not lecturing) why his behavior is inappropriate. Encourage your child to give other positive options that he believes will give him the result he wants, without hurting anyone.

To change his behavior, use discipline as a teaching tool. Rather than telling him not to hit his little brother, show him the correct and acceptable behavior that will resolve the conflict and prevent him from repeating the mistake.

*3. Be Kind, Yet Firm When Enforcing Discipline. Show Respect and Empathy*

A child may insist that what he did was right, hence the importance to enforce safety rules and consequences to prevent similar incidents in the future. Listen to his story as to why he did it and win half the battle by displaying empathy, but still impose the consequence of his action to make him learn from his mistakes. Empathy makes your child feel understood, lessening his resistance, and heightened emotions.

However, even when you are disciplining your child, be respectful and when you overreact, apologize. It will teach him to respect you more and the people around him. You should behave the way you want your child to behave while showing your parental authority.

Look for the "why" behind this behavior, especially when you observe that there is a pattern. Sometimes, hitting a sibling is a silent message that he is jealous of the attention you are giving to the younger child. Whatever the cause, resolve the issue early to make your child feels secure and loved. Treat the root cause and not the symptoms.

# Conclusion

Let's hope that this book was informative and able to provide you with all of the tools you need to achieve your goals whatever they may be.

The next step depends on you. If you are just starting off or in the early stages of preparation, take your time, and be sure that your child is really ready. Set your own pace and don't let it get you down if you come across a setback or regression. Children are resilient, and you need to be too. Commit to your child's success and be ready to drop everything when they need to get going quickly. Positive reinforcement is essential to long-term success.

Remember that parenting is not a marathon or a sprint. It requires time, practice, determination, the right skills, and perseverance to get the golden ticket—a respectful, well-mannered child. It is not a competition that you play with other parents. It is building a personal relationship with your child.

Parenting is about providing loving guidance with great purpose—to mold the character and personality of your child. It is about understanding who he is, what he cares about, what his dreams are, what brings him happiness or sadness, and what are his strengths and weaknesses. It is about focusing your time and attention on what matters to him while keeping limitations and boundaries.

Parenting is also learning about yourself as a nurturer, a disciplinarian, a confidant, and many other roles associated with it. If you make mistakes or feel your patience running out, take a time-out, and relax. You become a fine parent when you are happy, calm, and centered. Your health and well-being matter because it helps you become an objective, affectionate, and positive parent.

By being present and aware, your child is also empowering you and teaching you how to become a better person. When you know who you are, you become more capable of helping him understand himself. And when your child knows himself in the deepest sense, he is more confident to manage the challenges that come his way during his journey to adulthood. He can face the world with excitement and a purpose to contribute positively to make the world a better place to live

Finally, I wish you good luck for being a wonderful parent who believes that you need tools and guides to bring out the best in your child.